Real
Life

GUIDES

THE POLICE FORCE

REAL LIFE GUIDES

Practical guides for practical people

In this increasingly sophisticated world the need for manually skilled people to build our homes, cut our hair, fix our boilers, and make our cars go is greater than ever. As things progress, so the level of training and competence required of our skilled manual workers increases.

In this series of career guides from Trotman, we look in detail at what it takes to train for, get into, and be successful at a wide spectrum of practical careers. The *Real Life Guides* aim to inform and inspire young people and adults alike by providing comprehensive yet hard-hitting and often blunt information about what it takes to succeed in these careers.

The other titles in the series are:

Real Life Guide: the Armed Forces

Real Life Guide: the Beauty Industry

Real Life Guide: Carpentry & Cabinet-Making

Real Life Guide: Catering

Real Life Guide: Construction

Real Life Guide: Electrician

Real Life Guide: Hairdressing

Real Life Guide: the Motor Industry

Real Life Guide: Plumbing

Real Life Guide: Retailing

Real Life Guide: Working Outdoors

Real Life Guide: Working with Animals and Wildlife

Real Life Guide: Working with Young People

Real Life GUIDES

trotman

THE POLICE FORCE

Dee Pilgrim

Real Life Guide to the Police Force
This first edition published in 2005 by Trotman and Company Ltd
2 The Green, Richmond, Surrey TW9 1PL

© Trotman and Company Limited 2005

Editorial and Publishing Team
Author Dee Pilgrim
Editorial Mina Patria, Editorial Director; Rachel Lockhart,
Commissioning Editor; Catherine Travers, Managing Editor
Production Ken Ruskin, Head of Pre-Press and Production;
James Rudge, Production Artworker
Sales and Marketing Suzanne Johnson, Marketing
Manager
Advertising Tom Lee, Commercial Director

Designed by XAB

British Library Cataloguing in Publications Data
A catalogue record for this book is available from the British
Library

ISBN 1 84455 052 4

Typeset by Photoprint, Torquay
Printed and bound in Great Britain by
The Cromwell Press, Trowbridge, Wiltshire

Real
Life

GUIDES

CONTENTS

About the author

Dee Pilgrim studied journalism at the London College of Printing before working on a variety of music and women's titles. As a freelancer and a full-time member of staff she has written numerous articles and interviews for *Company*, *Cosmopolitan*, *New Woman*, *Woman's Journal* and *Weight Watchers* magazines. As a freelancer for Independent Magazines she concentrated on celebrity interviews and film, theatre and restaurant reviews for such titles as *Ms London*, *Girl About Town*, *LAM* and *Nine to Five* magazines, and in her capacity as a critic she has appeared on both radio and television. She is currently the Film Reviewer for *Now* magazine. When not attending film screenings she is active within the Critics' Circle, co-writes songs and is currently engaged in writing the narrative to an as-yet unpublished trilogy of children's illustrated books. She has written a variety of titles for Trotman Publishing including four other titles in the Real Life Guides series.

Acknowledgements

A huge thank you to Helen Kennedy and Dan Maskell of the Metropolitan Police Service's Press Office for help with interviews and arranging a day visit to the police training academy at Hendon. Steven Barrowclough of the Home Office's Crime Reduction and Community Safety Group provided essential information on the new Initial Police Learning and Development Programme. Thank you to Simon Lubin of the British Transport Police and Major Alan Faulkner of the Royal British Military Police for their help on these two related subjects. But, most importantly, many thanks to the officers who actually took the time and trouble to talk about their thoughts on the future of the police and on their own careers: Sir Ian Blair, Karen Killick, Louise McCarron, James Kew and Jonathan Morrison of the Metropolitan Police, and Brian McDonald and Lynne Hutchinson of Strathclyde Police.

Introduction

Police and thieves, cops and robbers, the Bill and the bad guys: whatever we choose to call them, it seems the British public is obsessed with law enforcement officers and the criminals they set out to catch. Bands sing songs about them, authors write best-selling books about them, actors clamour to play them in films, and if you turn on the television on any night of the week you'll be able to tune in to a programme about the police. Take, for example, one week in early summer 2005, when there were 19 prime time terrestrial television shows about the police and policing, ranging from documentary-style factual programmes (*World's Wildest Police Videos*, *Traffic Cops*) through dramas (*The Bill*, *55 Degrees North*) to shows dealing with work connected to police procedure (such as *CSI: Crime Scene Investigation*). It seems that the men and women who operate within the criminal investigation system fascinate us all.

For a lot of people that attraction and fascination is all about what they see as the 'glamour' of the job: the smart uniforms, fast car chases, the arrest of dangerous, perhaps famous criminals, and the subsequent high-profile court cases. But this is only a tiny part of what being a member of the police force is all about. In fact, the police play a much more important role in society than simply chasing villains. They are there to serve the community by protecting life and property, by preventing and investigating crime, by prosecuting offenders and by preserving order. People actually feel safer when they see 'bobbies' on the beat as their physical presence can decrease the risk of crime.

The police are there at the scenes of serious accidents, helping to keep traffic moving, comforting the injured and their relations and taking eyewitness accounts of what has happened. You will find them wherever there are large gatherings of people, such as sporting events, rallies and marches, making sure public order is maintained. If you are robbed or physically assaulted the police will investigate the crime and try to bring the perpetrator(s) to justice, while on Friday nights and at weekends they are on hand in large city centres to curtail drunken disorder. These are just some of the more visible roles taken by over 140,000 police officers in England and Wales, but the police often perform their duties out of the public eye – investigating international drug gangs, detecting serious fraud such as money-laundering, guarding against terrorist attacks and even protecting important members of state. No wonder we are so interested in what they do.

You'd think that, because their primary function is to help and protect all sections of the community, the police would be uniformly liked and respected – but this has not always been the case. Certain charges of brutality and corruption have caused some communities to view the police with suspicion. For example, in 1993 black teenager Stephen Lawrence was viciously murdered and the Metropolitan Police Service was accused of seriously mishandling the case. This led to the setting

DID YOU KNOW?

In April 2005, six years after ASBOs (Anti-Social Behaviour Orders) were first introduced, 1051 had been issued — that's roughly one every other day. The most interesting of these was against David Boag, a fan of the film 'American Werewolf in London', who was ordered not to howl like a wolf.

up of the Lawrence Inquiry whose report, published in 1999, accused the Met of being 'institutionally racist'. Steps were taken to address this issue. The Home Office amended the Race Relations Act and set a target of 5662 black and Asian officers to be serving in the police by 2009. Meanwhile, the Met set up a Community Safety Unit in every borough to record and investigate allegations of racism and other hate crimes.

Traditionally, the visible face of the force has been male and white. Now, in the same way as the country is moving towards a fully integrated multi-racial and multi-religious society, the make-up of the police force has changed. Of those 140,000 police officers, 20% are female and 3.3% (6.6% in the Metropolitan Police) are from minority ethnic backgrounds (source: the Home Office). The force is recruiting more and more people from all ethnic and social backgrounds and people from all communities are keen to join.

DID YOU KNOW?

Between 2000 and 2005 racist attacks in London fell by 35%. However, there were still 12,637 racist crimes recorded in London in 2004: that's 35 a day.

Source: Metropolitan Police.

The decision to become a police officer is not something you should take lightly. You need to think long and hard about whether this is something you really want to do. Although there are plenty of positive aspects to police work – the great variety in the work, good pay structure and opportunities for career progression – there are also the downsides, such as having to work shifts and the possibility of physical and verbal attack. About 10% of rank and file officers are attacked each year (source: www.police-information.co.uk). Policing is a serious

THE GAY POLICE ASSOCIATION

The Gay Police Association was formed in 1990. It has 2000 members across all the police forces in the UK and is the only national organisation that specifically represents the needs and interests of gay staff in the police. The aims of the association are to:

- Work towards equal opportunities for lesbian and gay police service employees
- Offer advice and support to lesbian and gay police service employees
- Promote better relations between the police service and the lesbian and gay community.

The GPA works in partnership with police forces, staff associations (eg the Police Federation) and other non-statutory staff associations (eg the National Black Police Association and the British Association for Women in Policing).

- Since 2003, uniformed police officers have taken part in lesbian and gay pride parades in London, Manchester and Brighton.
- GPA members work with police forces to help them deliver appropriate services to gay communities across the UK.
- Following the Soho bomb in 1999, GPA members were deployed to help interview witnesses and reassure the community.
- The GPA assists many forces with training police officers and staff so they can improve the service they deliver.

job, so you have to be serious about wanting to do it. You also have to be aware of just why you want to do it – if your prime motive is to swan around and play the hero rather than to do something positive for your community then you are not going to get very far. The rigorous police psychometric tests you have to undertake when applying to join are there to weed out those who are not emotionally or mentally equipped for the job. Nationally only 1 in 7 people succeeds in their application to be a police officer (source: www.police-information.co.uk).

But what qualifications do you need before you can even apply? What skills and talents help you to be a successful police officer? Even more important, what would becoming a police officer mean to you personally in terms of career development, financial benefits and social standing within your own community? This book is here to help you decide whether policing is really for you. It will explain exactly what a police officer is and what he or she does. It will also give you a better idea of the great variety of positions within the police and what specific skills you need for each of them. Real life case studies will show you what serving officers actually think about their jobs. Finally, it will explain what the police training entails. Reading this book will give you a better understanding about the police and policing and help you to make an informed decision about joining the force. Not everyone has the right mental attitude or social skills to make a success of a career in the police, so read on to discover whether or not you are one of the few who do.

This book is divided into 13 chapters. The table below gives you a brief guide to help you locate the information you need.

Nationally only 1 in 7 people succeeds in their application to be a police officer.

Chapter	Content	Page number

SIR IAN BLAIR QPM, MA

Success story

METROPOLITAN POLICE COMMISSIONER

Sir Ian has had a long and distinguished career with the Metropolitan Police in London, although during his time as Commissioner he has had to make some very difficult decisions. This was particularly true during the period of the London terrorist bombings in July 2005, when Sir Ian and his force were under huge pressure to protect members of the public while tracking down and apprehending members of terrorist cells. The need to respond in situations like this shows just how much responsibility the top jobs in the Police Force carry.

In 1974, after taking a degree in English Language and Literature at Oxford University, Sir Ian Blair joined the Police's Graduate Entry Scheme, becoming a Police Constable in Soho. From there he moved up through the ranks to become Detective Chief Inspector with the CID (Criminal Investigation Department) at Kentish Town, during which time he was responsible for the identification of victims of the King's Cross rail disaster. He then became Superintendent of Kensington

Policing is not a job; it is a vocation.

Division, and finally Chief Superintendent and Staff Officer to Her Majesty's Chief Inspector of Constabulary based at the Home Office. In 1993, he returned to the Met, at which point he was the officer in charge of Operation Gallery, one of London's largest ever police corruption enquiries.

In 1994, he became Assistant Chief Constable of Thames Valley Police, in 1998 Chief Constable of Surrey and eventually returned to the Metropolitan Police in 2000 when he became Deputy Commissioner and eventually Commissioner in February 2005. Sir Ian is committed to bringing about reform within the police service and the criminal justice system, and he has been instrumental in developing the position of Police Community Support Officers (PCSOs), of whom there are now 5000.

'In my opinion, policing is not a job; it is a vocation. The principal quality you need to succeed is an interest in people and an ability to empathise with them. At the same time, police officers have to be pretty unflappable and capable of taking control of situations when everyone else is getting a little frayed at the edges. Police officers require integrity, commitment and an appetite for hard work. There's also an absolute necessity for a sense of humour – an ability to see the positive in even the most trying of circumstances. You have to be organised and part of that organisation must be a decent work/life balance. Families and friends are a very important part of the support network and must be nurtured. The most successful officers are also often gifted with the ability to "think outside the box" – to understand logic but sometimes to go with intuition.

'I have been a police officer for 30 years and, because policing is really about human behaviour, it is still broadly the same as it ever was, except the threats of personal violence towards officers are much worse. Also, many people now look to the police to deal with anti-social behaviour, as well as crime. At the same time, the threat of international terrorism has produced a new dimension for policing – but improvements in equipment and training and the growth in numbers of police officers themselves have hugely improved our ability to live up to these challenges.

We have officers dealing with graffiti in Barking and Kingston and others on the ground in Baghdad and Kabul.

'My job is to lead an enormous organisation, with a proud history, into the twenty-first century and I feel very honoured to have been chosen to take command of such an extraordinary organisation with such an extraordinary mission. The police service reflects the community it serves and it has faced problems of racism and sexism and other forms of discrimination, in common with other public institutions. However, looking at the Met at the moment, we are the largest employer of women and of minorities in London. Nearly 20% of last year's recruits were from minority communities and we are gradually making the Metropolitan Police Service a better reflection of London's diverse population. Also, the standard of police recruits from all communities has risen and is still rising.

'I can say I honestly enjoy every day [of my job]. I particularly like having the opportunity to meet the brave and talented men and women who make up this service and listen to their concerns and achievements. I enjoy meeting those who are joining and hearing of their commitment to public service and I endeavour to see some of those retiring to thank them for what they have done. It would be wonderful if we could get away from the rather limited image of policing portrayed in the media because the police mission is ever-widening. We have officers dealing with graffiti in Barking and Kingston and others on the ground in Baghdad and Kabul.

'This is a fantastic and exciting profession, intellectually challenging and full of the requirement to show personal leadership. My best piece of advice for anyone who wants to join the police is to ensure they see a bit of life beforehand. The average age for people to join the police in London is now the mid-twenties and I think that provides people with an understanding of the complexities and ambiguities of life. It provides them with an ability to communicate and to understand the points of view of others and what motivates people and communities. Every day, across London and everywhere else in Britain, men and women put their own lives at risk for others. I think it is fantastic that people volunteer to do this job.'

What's all this then?

The days of the friendly local bobby in uniform walking slowly down the street, stopping to say 'evening all' to everyone he meets may seem to belong to a bygone age, but much of what police do now is the same as when the blueprint for our modern police force was first set up nearly 200 years ago. That was when Home Secretary Sir Robert Peel set out to overhaul and reform the penal code (ie the codes concerning punishment of criminals), giving rise to Britain's first 'bobbies' or 'peelers'.

Because we've all grown up with a properly maintained and trained police force it's almost impossible to believe there was a time when the police did not exist, although the people of Britain have had systems for keeping law and order since Saxon times. At that time a 'tithing-man', responsible for a group of ten people, had to answer to the Shire-reeve (Sheriff) of his shire or county if any of the group caused unrest. This system gradually evolved over the years until tithing-men became parish constables who were elected annually to serve (unpaid) for a year, while the Sheriff became the Justice of the Peace.

As the population of Britain grew, so too did the size of towns and the amount of crime being committed in them. So parish constables evolved again, this time into the 'Watch', who were paid for guarding the town gates, patrolling the streets at night and even lighting streetlamps. However, the beginning of the eighteenth century and the Industrial Revolution saw the populations of our towns and cities soaring and it became clear that a properly co-ordinated force to uphold law and order was needed. In 1742 London got the Bow Street Runners, although soldiers were still being used to quell riots and mass disorder. It wasn't until 1829 that the Metropolitan Police Act was passed and the first of Peel's police were seen on the streets of London. At first there were just 1000 policemen, who were paid 16 shillings a week and were based at Scotland Yard. To join, you had to be six feet (1.83 metres) tall with no history of any wrongdoing and be prepared to work seven days a week.

DID YOU KNOW?

The first ever police office in a shop in London opened at the Eltham branch of the Co-op in April 2005. It is used as a base by six local officers who patrol the area on bicycles and on foot.

Source: Metropolitan Police

After initial resentment and distrust from the public, these forerunners of our modern police soon proved their worth. However, it still took some time for other areas around the country to get their own forces – by 1855 there were only 12,000 policemen in the whole of England and Wales. In 1856 parliament mandated that all provinces had to establish police forces and also made provision for government inspection, audit and regulation of those forces. The era of modern policing had truly begun.

Now there are over 214,365 full-time staff working in the police service in England and Wales, and of these roughly 66% (140,000) are police officers. The make-up of the police has also changed drastically. You no longer need to be a six-foot, white male to join. Women comprise 20% (28,209) of police officers, while 3.3% (4629) of officers are from minority ethnic backgrounds.

These days there is also a wider, extended police family. Although special constables (unpaid volunteers) have been around for over 150 years, the Police Act of 1964 really established the Special Constabulary in its present form and now every force in England and Wales has its own Special Constabulary with nearly 11,000 serving specials in total. A newer development has been the introduction of police community support officers (PCSOs) as a result of the Police Reform Act 2002. PCSOs provide assistance to the police but do not have full police powers. There are currently over 3400 PCSOs with a nationwide target of 4000 set for March 2006 (source: the Home Office).

DID YOU KNOW?

Strathclyde Police was the first UK force to achieve Investors in People status and employs over 2000 support staff including clerical and administrative staff as well as drivers, forensic experts, vehicle technicians and communication operators.

Source: Strathclyde Police Force

As a police officer you really can make a difference to society as a whole.

Today the duties of officers are much more varied than they would have been during the Victorian era, but the first of Sir Robert Peel's Nine Principles of Policing still holds true. It says that 'the basic mission for which the police exist is to prevent crime and disorder'. Add to this protecting life and property, assisting at fires and accidents (especially road accidents),

DID YOU KNOW?

The BAWP (British Association for Women in Policing) was set up in 1987 and is the only organisation in the UK to embrace women of all ranks and grades within the police service. Its main objective is to enhance the role and understanding of the specific needs of women within the police. It works to contribute to the continuous professional development of all its members, to raise awareness and understanding of issues affecting women in the service, and to develop a network of professional and social contacts between officers nationally and internationally.

Source: www.bawp.org

taking statements, arresting suspects, giving evidence in court, maintaining national security, supporting victims and even having to inform relatives about the deaths of crime or accident victims and you can see just how demanding the role of the modern police officer is. However, it is also very rewarding because as a police officer you really can make a difference to society as a whole. Whether you are walking the street, patrolling in a police car, giving a talk in a school, maintaining order at a football game or attending the scene of a crime, members of the public know they can approach you for anything from asking for directions to getting assistance if they have been assaulted.

You need to be really committed to make a good police officer and you also need special skills and talents. For many people the shift working pattern of the modern police and the responsibilities of being an officer prove too much. However, this does not mean there is no place for them within today's police force. In Chapter 4 we look in more detail at what being an officer actually entails and the kind of strengths and abilities that can help you to make a successful career in the police, and in Chapter 6 we will discuss in detail other jobs in the police force that suit different people's personal characteristics.

LYNNE HUTCHINSON
POLICE SUPERINTENDENT

Case study 1

Lynne studied to become a primary school teacher after doing her Highers in Scotland. However, when she qualified she took a postgraduate diploma in Careers Guidance and worked as a Careers Adviser for nearly five years. It was when she was studying for an Open University degree in Social Sciences that she met some police officers and seriously started to consider joining the police. Up to this point she did not feel she had the stomach for it, but with the encouragement of one of the officers she applied for the force and was successful. She is now working in the personnel department of Strathclyde Police headquarters.

'I was 26 years old at the time and a bit fed up with my job so I thought it was worth taking the chance, even though I wasn't sure if I could actually do it. But there's plenty of on-the-job training. When you join any of the Scottish forces you go to the Scottish Police College for two residential courses during your first two years to learn about legislation and police powers, and to improve your fitness levels. Then there's a variety of training after that.

It's very much a team job, working together to solve problems and relying on one another's support.

I have to re-qualify annually in my officer safety equipment – baton, handcuffs and CS spray – and in first aid.

'I have progressed fairly quickly in the police service because I was successful in applying for the Accelerated Promotion Scheme after I had about seven years' service. I actually joined to be a constable but have loved every minute of my career, each promotion has been a bonus and I'm delighted at achieving the rank of Superintendent.

'At present I work in personnel and one of my main functions is to supervise the career development of officers, so I hold promotion interviews and select officers for promoted posts, which is very rewarding. Most police officers join because they want to be part of the local community and for the variety of different situations they have to face but, in the position I hold now, the thing I like the most is being involved in the development of others, ensuring they have the opportunity to progress in the service as I have done myself. The advice for young people used to be to join later in life after undertaking higher education or obtaining another trade. This was to encourage applicants when they were more mature. However, maturity doesn't necessarily come with age and I would advise people to apply when they feel the time is right. I would say to anyone considering policing as a career: make the most of it! Whether you aspire to promotion, to lateral development, to one of the many specialised posts or to remain as a patrol officer, the opportunities are there for you. I would encourage school leavers to join the Cadets because the training gives you great insight into the police service. Many of our cadets go straight into the regular force when they are 18 and a half.

'You will need good people skills to be able to handle the public in the variety of situations you will come across, from controlling a crowd to persuading someone to follow your instructions, or comforting victims. It's very much a team job, working together to solve problems and relying on one another's support in dangerous and difficult situations. However, I can't think of any downsides to what I do. Yes, it would be nice to be able to clear all the work from my desk at Personnel at the end of the day but that's about it.'

The (un)usual suspects

Some people are lucky in that they know from a young age exactly what they want to be when they grow up. If you are an extremely talented artist it's probable you will go on to have a career in the arts, or if science is your thing you'll probably use it in the future in your job. But there are so many different jobs within the police, and you need so many different skills that knowing whether you are a suitable candidate is tricky. However, you could start by finding out if your idea of what a police officer is and does is realistic or a total fantasy you've created from the numerous depictions of the police you've seen in the media. Take a few minutes to do the quick quiz below to see just how much you really know about the police. Once you've done that, have a look at the list of abilities you should be bringing to a career in the police force – some of them might surprise you. Finally, look at the list of things that could bar you from being an officer. Then be honest with yourself; have you really got what it takes to get through the gruelling police probationary period?

Police quiz

Because we see police officers on the streets and in television programmes and films almost every day, most of us think we have a pretty good idea about what they do, how far their powers go and what makes good police practice. In reality, however, it's surprising just how little we actually do know. The following quiz is a fun way to test your knowledge of the police. The early questions are all factually based, whereas those that come later are designed to see how you would react in certain police situations and whether or not that reaction is appropriate. This will give you a better idea of whether you have what it takes to make a success of a job in the force. After each question just tick the answer you believe to be correct.

1. What is the minimum height requirement for a male to join the police?

    A. 6 feet (1.83 metres).
    B. 5 feet 8 inches (1.73 metres).
    C. There is no height requirement.

2. What is the minimum age requirement to join the police in England and Wales?

    A. 20 years old.
    B. $18^1/_2$ years old.
    C. 21 years old.

3. Which of the following is not standard police issue?

    A. A baton.
    B. A firearm.
    C. CS spray.

4. How many police services are there in England, Northern Ireland and Wales?

   A. 43.
   B. 17.
   C. 54.

5. What is a police constable allowed to do that a police community support officer cannot?

   A. Search a vehicle.
   B. Make an arrest.
   C. Issue a fixed penalty ticket for a minor offence.

For questions 6–10, try to put yourself in the position of a police officer dealing with each of the situations described. What would you do?

6. You have been called to the scene of a car crash in which a young person has been injured. He is pronounced dead by the ambulance crew. The parents need to be informed. Do you:

   A. Get someone else to do it?
   B. Say their son is in hospital but they'll have to ask the doctors how badly injured he is?
   C. Explain quietly, calmly and with sympathy what has happened, expressing your own sorrow at their loss?

7. You are called to a robbery at a local post office. When you arrive the gang is just getting away by car; one of them looks like he may have a gun. Do you:

   A. Pursue the getaway car in your patrol vehicle, hoping to cut them off and catch them?

  B. Pursue the getaway car but immediately call your
     control room for armed back-up?
  C. Pursue the getaway car, call for back-up, saying you
     think one of them may be armed, and keep
     monitoring the situation until you can be sure whether
     a firearm is involved?

8. You arrest a suspected thief who has a quantity of
   prescription drugs on him. As you move to confiscate
   them he tells you they are for a serious medical condition
   and he cannot be without them. Do you:

  A. Take them away anyway – they might be stolen?
  B. Let him keep them – without them he could get
     seriously sick?
  C. Consult the police doctor to see if it is safe to leave
     them with him?

9. While out on patrol one day you are stopped by a local
   resident complaining about a gang of young kids causing
   a nuisance in the area. He points them out to you and it
   is clear they are acting in an anti-social manner. Do you:

  A. Tell them to clear off, warning them that if they return
     you'll serve them with an Anti-Social Behaviour Order
     (ASBO)?
  B. Go over and talk to them, telling them their behaviour
     is not acceptable and getting their names and
     addresses for future reference?
  C. Immediately serve them with an ASBO?

10. There has been some vandalism at a row of local shops
    and one of the shopkeepers is threatening to take
    matters into his own hands. Do you:

A. Tell him this is not a good idea and show him you are taking the matter seriously by talking it through with him and discussing crime prevention measures he could take?

B. Let him get on with it – the vandals are a nuisance to everyone in the area?

C. Immediately arrest him – this is a police matter and he mustn't be allowed to interfere?

ANSWERS

1. **C**. When the Metropolitan Police Act was passed in 1829 the first peelers (constables) had to be six feet (1.83 metres) tall or as near as possible, and male. However, today these restrictions don't apply, so if you are a five-foot (1.52 metres) female you can still join.

2. **B**. The minimum age is 18 and a half, but if you are over 16 you can join the Police Cadets, which is a good way to see whether a job in policing suits you or not. Although there is no real upper age limit for joining the police in England and Wales, in Scotland the upper age limit is 40. (There is more information about the Cadets in Chapter 12; also see Resources (Chapter 13).)

3. **B**. All police constables are issued with protective vests, handcuffs, a baton and CS spray but they do not, as a matter of course, carry guns. Although, due to the terrorist attacks in July 2005, people are seeing more armed police on the street, the UK in fact has one of only very few unarmed police forces in the world. In situations where an

armed response is called for, a member of a firearms unit, specially trained in handling weapons, will be brought in.

4. **A (or C)**. There are currently 43 police forces in England, Northern Ireland and Wales. (If you also take into account Scotland, the Isle of Man and the Channel Islands there are 54.) However, in September 2005 the Home Secretary proposed a reduction in the number of Police Forces, which is now being looked into.

5. **B**. Unlike police constables, community support officers do not have the power of arrest. However, they can detain a person for up to 30 minutes pending the arrival of a police officer (this is similar to the power of 'Citizen's Arrest' which we all have). Another difference between PCSOs and police constables is the equipment they carry: PCSOs wear uniform but they do not carry handcuffs, batons or CS spray.

6. **C**. Being a police officer requires maturity because having to inform families of victims about serious injuries and even deaths is part of the job. If you don't think you could handle having to give people bad news then maybe the police force is not the place for you.

7. **C**. When you become a police officer you have to accept that inevitably you will find yourself in potentially life-threatening situations. However, this does not mean you have to take unnecessary risks. Getting yourself killed while trying to be a hero (A) is just plain stupid, while calling out a firearms unit without good cause (B) is a waste of resources. A good officer would monitor the situation, keeping in contact with their control room at all times and requesting back-up as and when the need arises.

8. **C**. This question is based on a true-life situation, when an officer still on probation let an arrested man keep what he claimed to be prescribed medication. The man, a drug addict, then proceeded to swallow the whole bottle of pills, effectively overdosing and requiring a trip to hospital to have his stomach pumped. The man survived but he could just as easily have died. When in doubt, ask someone who knows. In this case that would be the police doctor.

9. **B**. Telling a bunch of rowdy kids to clear off may make them move in the short term, but as soon as the police officers continue on their beat they are almost sure to return. Taking names and addresses means you can check up on them if their behaviour is a cause for concern in the future. Then, once they have been warned and have ignored the warning, the time is right to issue an ASBO.

10. **A**. The shopkeeper is obviously very distressed about what has been happening at his premises, but taking the law into his own hands is not the way to go. He needs your reassurance that you are taking his grievances seriously – you could do this by making detailed notes of the dates, times and nature of the vandalism. He also needs constructive advice on how to stop the vandals – so talking through crime prevention measures (such as installing a CCTV camera) would be helpful. Sometimes, your job in the force may be to show your support by simply sitting and listening to members of your local community.

Count up how many of the above questions you got right. Remember that what's important is not how much you know now but how much potential you have to develop the skills you'll need while out on the beat. The ability to solve problems and be decisive are just two of the strengths a good police officer needs. Some of these skills may seem obvious, but there are others you may not even have considered that are just as important. The paragraphs below should give you an idea of some of the most important personal qualities and abilities you can bring to a career in the police.

COMMON SENSE

You need to be methodical and accurate so an ability to think logically is a must and this ties in with having a good deal of common sense. If you spend your time daydreaming on the job then you're not going to be of any use to anybody.

COMMUNICATION SKILLS

As a member of the police you will be talking to other officers and to members of the public all the time. You need to make yourself clearly understood and to get instructions across with the minimum of fuss. You may be talking to an elderly member of the public on the street, relaying information to your control centre via the radio, giving evidence in court, or even giving talks to children in schools. What you say and how you say it matters and you will have to learn to adapt the way you talk depending on your audience – talking to the victims of crime requires different communication skills to talking to a drunk who could get violent. If the thought of all that talking makes your mouth dry and fills you with dread then you are going to find it hard to do your job effectively.

CONFIDENCE

Self-confidence is a bonus whatever job you are going to do, but in the police force it's a must. For a start you need to be able to approach people from all walks of life, sometimes under threatening circumstances. Calming down an inflammatory situation becomes even harder if you feel intimidated yourself. Standing up in court reading out evidence can test the nerve of even the most self-assured of people and if you don't have the confidence to make decisions under pressure you will find your work suffering. The training for probationary officers will help to build your confidence, but this is a personal quality you really need to have before you start.

DISCIPLINE
Just as there is no place for dishonesty in the police force, there is also no place for ill-discipline. Hollywood films might like to show us cops who are mavericks or loose cannons (such as Mel Gibson in the *Lethal Weapon* series), but the reality is that if every police officer did their own thing there would be no law and order. You must be willing and able to obey orders and to follow the strict letter of the law – inability to adhere to correct police procedure could mean court cases being thrown out on technicalities and could also threaten your career prospects within the force. You will also need to adopt a disciplined approach to the administration involved in your job – even officers on the beat have to fill in forms.

DRIVING LICENCE
Here's something else you might never have considered, but it makes sense when you do. Although the police force has its own driving schools (to teach advanced driving skills such as those needed for high-speed pursuits), having a full driving licence when you join (or at least having started taking lessons) will put you at an advantage over someone who does not know how to drive.

HONESTY

You may not be very surprised to see 'honesty' in this list: surely it goes without saying. But honesty is about more than just being honest with others – it is also about having the ability to be honest with yourself. For example, in certain situations do you make decisions on the evidence in front of you, or are you being swayed by your own prejudices or even because a certain decision makes your life easier? If you know you are inclined to think some people are more likely to commit crime because of their race, age, sex, social standing or religious beliefs, your ability to deal with all sections of society fairly and honestly will be compromised. Before you even think about joining the police, here's a question to test your honesty: do you want to join the police because you like the idea of wearing a uniform and being in a position of authority that allows you to boss people about, or because you really want to put something back into your community, preventing crime and protecting life and property? Remember, there is no place in the police force for dishonest officers.

MENTAL MATURITY

Even if you join the police at a relatively young age you will have to demonstrate that you are mature enough to handle the rigours of the job. You need to be able to stay calm under pressure, make decisions quickly and use common sense. If you make mistakes you have to take responsibility for them and rectify them. If you don't want all that responsibility this may not be the job for you.

OBSERVATIONAL SKILLS

Court cases often rely on police evidence for prosecutions and so your powers of observation need to be strong.

Exactly what colour was the shirt of the vandal you saw throwing that brick? What was the registration number of the stolen car in Long Road? Not only do you need to notice and remember facts and details, you also need to be able to record them accurately. Your ability to gather information must be reliable, and this is another way in which discipline, this time mental discipline, plays its part.

PATIENCE

Some cases take years to solve. Suspects must be eliminated, new evidence may come to light and police officers will patiently have to sift through it all, building up a 'bigger picture' of the crime. You cannot afford to lose patience with a case because this is when vital information can get overlooked, or the relevance of a statement can be missed.

PHYSICAL FITNESS

Your personal fitness is important not only to you, but also to your fellow officers. What if you have to chase a suspect or restrain someone who is being violent? If a fellow officer is under attack, do you have the physical strength to help restrain the attacker? If there's a fight going on outside a football ground, do you have both the courage and physical ability to intervene? More likely than not you will be out and about on your feet for most of a routine day and so a good level of health and fitness is essential. In fact, prospective officers must pass physical fitness and medical entrance tests before being accepted and poor fitness levels are a major cause for candidates being rejected.

RESPECT FOR YOUR COMMUNITY

The police are there to protect the whole of society, not just a chosen few, so good police officers are those who have

The police are there to protect the whole of society, not just a chosen few.

respect for others' beliefs and points of view. Getting to know everyone in your community and building relationships with community leaders will help you to do your job. You need to be able to show tolerance and be tactful.

SENSE OF HUMOUR
This is one quality you might not have even thought about when considering the police as a career, but if you want this to be a job for life, you really do need to keep a sense of humour. You will be dealing with serious issues every day, and if you feel you are not making headway against crime and disorder it can really get you down. You need to be able to laugh and to keep a sense of perspective, because disillusionment can lead to people leaving the force prematurely.

TEAMWORK
Although you should be able to show you can work independently using your own initiative, you really have to be a team player to be a member of the police. This means building good working relationships with your fellow officers and ensuring you are functioning as a unit. If you are a diehard loner then this really isn't the job for you because people need to know they can rely on you when things get tough.

OTHER THINGS TO CONSIDER
If the above are all strengths you need to bring to the job, it goes without saying that weaknesses in these areas could

well hold you back. **Lack of physical fitness** is one of the biggest hurdles to cross and this includes good eyesight and colour vision (with or without glasses or contact lenses). Tied in with this is **lack of stamina**. If you are working as a police officer you will be on shifts and these will include night shifts. Not only can this be physically exhausting but it can play havoc with your home life and social life. Remember that while others are out on the town at the weekend, you could well be in a patrol car making sure drunken fights don't break out in city centres. If you want a nine-to-five existence you won't find it as a police constable.

Any form of **prejudice** (including racial, gender, sexual orientation and religious) will not be tolerated within the police, nor will an **inability to follow orders** from a superior officer. If you don't like being bossed around and have a problem with authority figures then this really isn't for you. Finally, if you have any sort of **criminal conviction**, even for something you think is quite trivial, you *must* declare it when you apply to join the police. There are some convictions that will immediately make you unsuitable for the job, and don't think that you can get away with it by keeping quiet – you will always get found out!

The huge variety of job opportunities available is one of the reasons many people join the police force.

Now you've read about the qualities you need to make it in the police you are probably realising just why it takes an induction course and a further two years of probation before a constable is fully qualified. If that sounds like a long, hard grind that's not for you, you could still find another job within the police. There are 73,802 staff in supporting roles within the police (source: the Home Office), including traffic wardens, crime scene investigators, call controllers and secretarial staff, so there are positions for everybody, whatever their abilities and interests. In fact, the huge variety of job opportunities available is one of the reasons many people join the police force in the first place. In Chapter 6 (Whodunnit?) we look at the range of roles available.

RANKS IN THE POLICE

Rank	Approximate numbers
CONSTABLES	112,407
SERGEANTS	19,523
INSPECTORS	6616
CHIEF INSPECTORS	1887
SUPERINTENDENTS	948
CHIEF SUPERINTENDENTS	540
ASSOCIATION OF CHIEF POLICE OFFICERS (ACPO) RANKS – ASSISTANT CHIEF CONSTABLE, DEPUTY CHIEF CONSTABLE AND CHIEF CONSTABLE	224

Source: the Home Office

5

JAMES KEW

Case study 2

MOUNTED POLICEMAN WITH THE MET

James joined the police eight years ago when he was 23 years old. He had always wanted to be a policeman, but after doing A levels he became a fitness instructor so he could get more experience of meeting people. He then trained at Hendon Police Academy and was posted first to Wimbledon and later to Mitcham in South London. From here he transferred – or was 'compulsory tendered' – to Brixton, where there was a shortage of officers. He finally made the decision to join the Mounted Branch in late 2003 and went to Imber Court in Esher, which is the training centre not only for mounted police but also for the horses they will eventually ride. After a 16-week intensive training course he 'passed out' (completed his training) in January 2004. There are eight mounted divisions across the whole of the Metropolitan area and James is posted in Wandsworth (in south-west London), where there are fifteen horses tended to by two sergeants, fifteen constables and two civilian staff who help with the general

You need to be good at management, organised, a team player and a good communicator welfare and everyday working of the stables. James rides a police horse called Brigadier.

'It all happened because my wife introduced me to horses and I decided I wanted to work with them. Also, I like public order work and that's really our bread and butter in the mounted division, so joining made perfect sense.

'I could ride when I started but I was still a novice and I would say to anyone wanting to join the mounted police: spend some time around horses and do some riding beforehand because if you haven't done that then it's a big surprise when you come off a horse for the first time! Nearly everyone does come off at some point: I came off three times while at Imber Court. The training is physically and mentally very tiring because you have to learn about the whole shebang – not just about riding, but about the management of horses, their welfare, what workload they can take, the care of the kit – everything.

'Because we are a public order branch we get to work anywhere where there are crowds, from carnivals such as the Notting Hill Carnival, to football and rugby matches, and large marches. It's said that a mounted officer is as good as 12 officers on their feet because we are elevated and we've got a really good view on crowds and crowd dynamics. In the worst-case scenario, which is riots, we are pretty much the last line of defence.

'A typical day for me starts at 7am when I get to the stables, check the horses to see if they are all right from the night before, feed them, groom them, check our kit, check the stables and then check which route I am taking that day depending on what has been going on. For instance, there has been a big robbery in Wandsworth recently and so we will patrol that area to reassure the public – it's called a high visibility patrol. We will leave the stables at about 11am in what we call 'cross section' which basically means in pairs. You wouldn't believe the number of people who come up to the horses – it's fantastic because it breaks down the barriers between the police and the community. The ride will probably last about two hours before we come back, make sure the horses are comfortable, give them their hay and then do our police reports.

'The things I like most about what I do are working with my fellow officers – we are a close-knit team here – working with the horses and working with the public. Police work is very varied and I enjoy that, but I suppose the main thing is working with the horses because they are lovely creatures. It is hard physically and

We are a close-knit team here.

some people do get injured; in fact I've just returned from a shoulder injury, but apart from that I don't think there are any downsides to this job: I really enjoy what I do.

'You need to be good at management, organised, a team player and a good communicator to make a success of this career but you don't necessarily have to come from a 'horsey' background. I actually have my own horse on which I go one-day eventing but that is the exception rather than the norm in the mounted division. I want to continue here. I can progress by doing an Intermediate Course to help me train young horses and then go on to the Instructor's Course where I learn to train student riders. I certainly see myself staying in the mounted police for a long time.'

6

Whodunnit?

In this chapter we take a look at who does what in the police force. The bobby on the beat and the patrol officer in their police car may be the most common faces of the police we see in everyday life, but they are by no means the only roles the police play. As we saw earlier there are dozens of different jobs in law enforcement, each needing different skills and abilities. Some you may already be familiar with, but others may be quite new to you. Below are some of the positions available in the police and also those that are most closely related to them.

POLICE OFFICER

Since the first days of the peelers, police officers have been responsible for maintaining law and order, detecting and preventing crime and bringing criminals to justice. Police officers carry out their duties in a variety of different ways and in many locations. They may be out on patrol – on foot, on a bicycle, in a patrol car or even on horseback – or they may be based permanently at a school, or working in front of a computer, or at the front desk of a police station. Some days they may be drafted in to police special events such as football matches, rock concerts or even royal weddings!

Police officers conduct searches, take statements, make arrests, attend crime scenes and accidents, and must even give evidence in court. Most officers work a 40-hour week, which normally includes shift work and working some weekends and public holidays such as Christmas. To become a police officer you must be $18^1/_2$ years or over and must pass rigorous medical and fitness tests before completing a residential training course and then a two-year probationary period.

Many officers love the variety of being on the beat so much they choose to remain there for the whole of their careers. However, others decide to receive further training in order to have a specialised role within a specific area. These include:

AIR SUPPORT UNITS

Sometimes it is just not possible for the police to do their job 'on the ground': they need increased visibility from planes or, more frequently, from helicopters in order to get a full picture of what is going on. It could be that they are helping a unit on the ground to chase a stolen car or a suspect on foot at night. In this situation they use special thermal imaging equipment in order to see what the naked human eye cannot.

CRIMINAL INVESTIGATION DEPARTMENT (CID)

Apparently, one in eight of all police staff is an officer engaged in detective work. Detectives are plain-clothes police officers, and are ranked within the normal police hierarchy, eg detective constable, detective sergeant. Paperwork (much of which is carried out by computer these days) and surveillance take up a lot of a detective's time and

DID YOU KNOW?

Security arrangements for the marriage of Prince Charles to Camilla Parker Bowles at Windsor in April 2005 involved over 550 officers from Thames Valley Police Authority as well as several hundred officers from the Metropolitan Police drafted in to guard the royal family and its VIP guests. The cost of policing the event was estimated at £2 million.

Source: Evening Standard

you must be able to pay meticulous attention to detail in order to be a successful detective. You could be working for the Fraud Squad.

DOG HANDLERS

The police force now employs dogs in a variety of different ways. They help maintain order at football matches and at large rallies. They sniff out and catch criminals and increasingly they are used to detect drugs and explosives: you will often see police dogs and their handlers checking luggage at large airports. If you like dogs (and some experience with dogs is a bonus) this may be a job you could pursue – but remember, police dogs live with their handlers who are responsible for their welfare. Competition for places as a dog handler is fierce and there are usually long waiting lists. In time and with more training you could go on to become a police dog trainer.

DRUGS SQUADS

Criminal dealings in drugs have increased greatly in recent years and now many officers are involved with tracking down drugs entering this country and keeping dealers under surveillance. Some drug squad operations involve forces from overseas as well as those in the UK and may take months to set up.

FIREARMS UNITS

In this country there are very stringent rules in place about when and where police may use firearms. Members of the firearms units are professionally trained and are called in to assist only in specific circumstances such as hostage situations, during times of heightened national security or when armed members of the public are proving a danger to other civilians, the police, or both. As a member of a firearms unit you may be called upon to shoot to kill, so a decision to join should not be taken lightly.

THE FRAUD SQUAD
Fraud, especially credit card and internet fraud, is one of the areas where criminal activity has mushroomed in recent years and increasing numbers of officers are now employed in tackling it. People often talk about fraud as being a 'victimless' crime but this is not true. If someone steals your identity in order to empty your bank account, your bank may reimburse you for what you have lost, but we all have to pay in the long run through higher bank charges and insurance premiums. Many officers who work in the area of fraud have very specialised computer skills.

MOUNTED POLICE
You don't necessarily need to know how to ride in order to join the Mounted Branch, but it definitely helps, if only to give you some idea of what it feels like to take a fall (see the Case Study on Mounted Policeman James Kew in Chapter 5). Even if you do know how to ride you will have to complete a riding course at the special school at Imber Court, Esher. The mounted police are most involved in keeping public order, which is why you will see them at events where there are large crowds (demonstrations, rallies, sporting events): this is because they are highly visible and indicate clearly that there is a police presence.

NATIONAL CRIME SQUAD/NATIONAL CRIMINAL INTELLIGENCE SERVICE
Where crime is organised on a national scale, the National Crime Squad will co-ordinate proceedings with local forces,

questioning contacts, organising surveillance and making sure everyone knows what everyone else is doing.

SPECIAL BRANCH
Special Branch handles any policing matters involving national security. This may be a visit by a head of state (such as the President of the United States), times when our own Prime Minister may be at risk or any occasions where terrorist attacks are likely to take place.

TRAFFIC POLICE
If you've ever seen any of the television programmes about traffic police you'll know this job is not just about high-speed chases in police cars or on motorbikes with flashing lights and blaring sirens; it's also about honing your observational skills so you can spot vehicles that are not roadworthy, have tax discs that are out of date, or have been stolen. And it's about watching out for drivers who are acting suspiciously or driving dangerously while under the influence of drink or other drugs. When you join the Traffic Police you will be given special tuition at a driving school.

UNDERWATER SEARCH UNITS
During large manhunts, where people have gone missing in suspicious circumstances, frogmen are often used to search in lakes, canals, rivers and even quarries. They may also be employed to find murder weapons or other evidence. In England and Wales there are now 22 underwater search units and officers are given specialised training in diving.

POLICE COMMUNITY SUPPORT OFFICER (PCSO)
The role of police community support officer has really been developing since the Police Reform Act of 2002. PCSOs deal with matters that don't need full police powers, such as

truancy, graffiti, littering and even abandoned vehicles, freeing up police time to deal with other matters. They wear uniforms and do shift work, including weekends, and are paid a salary for their work. To become a PCSO you must be at least 18 years old, pass a fitness test and undergo an intensive three-week induction course; from then on training is on the job. This can be a great way of finding out if a job as a police officer is really for you or if you want to help the community but do not want the full responsibility that being a constable involves. For more information visit www.national-pcsos.co.uk.

SPECIAL CONSTABLE

The Police Act of 1964 established the Special Constabulary as we now know it. Specials have the same powers as regular police and wear a similar uniform, but the main difference between them and police officers is that they are volunteers. They may have full-time or part-time jobs or be bringing up families and work as specials for at least four hours a week. Trained by local police forces, they take part in foot patrols, house-to-house enquiries and the presentation of evidence in court as well as the policing of major public events. Although not paid a salary, they are reimbursed for their expenses and if you are keen to make a practical contribution to keeping your local community crime-free, becoming a special is a great way to do so. It is also an excellent way to experience policing before deciding to become a police officer full-time. To find out more, have a look at the website www.specialconstables.gov.uk.

CRIME SCENE INVESTIGATION (CSI)

The enormous success of the various *CSI: Crime Scene Investigation* series on television has shown just how interested the public is in what actually goes on at the scenes of accidents, murders and other crimes. The role of forensics in detecting, recovering and examining evidence has become increasingly important as science can now be used to prosecute suspects. (It makes you wonder how they managed to solve crimes at all before fingerprinting and DNA analysis!)

Some people in forensics are employed directly by police forces but most are recruited by the Forensic Science Service (FSS), which in turn is employed by the police, the Ministry of Defence Police, the British Transport Police, the Crown Prosecution Service and HM Customs and Excise. Although a variety of jobs are mentioned below these are only some of the roles in CSI, and are those most closely related to the police – other, more specialised jobs (such as the role of coroner) belong in a book more closely geared to the sciences. Jobs in CSI include crime scene investigators and scenes of crime officers.

CRIME SCENE INVESTIGATOR/SCENES OF CRIME OFFICER
There are approximately 1800 crime scene examiners in the UK and competition for places is extremely fierce. Duties include protecting the crime scene from contamination, taking fingerprints, taking photographic and video evidence, examining prisoners for traces of evidence, storing and

Crime scene investigators work wherever a crime has taken place, so you could be on a motorway, in a house, in a country lane or even in a nightclub.

submitting exhibits of evidence to court, and even facial identification techniques. Crime scene investigators work wherever a crime has taken place, so you could be on a motorway, in a house, in a country lane or even in a nightclub. The work can be gruesome, involving bodies that have been cut, burnt or mutilated, so if the sight of blood makes you squeamish then this is definitely not the job for you. Once again, you will need a good level of fitness to cope with carrying and lifting equipment used on the job. There is no minimum entry age but because of the nature of the job most applicants are in their early 20s and some candidates study for a relevant degree in the sciences before applying.

DEPARTMENT OF FORENSIC MEDICAL SCIENCES

This is very specialised work dealing with autopsies and clinical forensic medicine, especially where cases of medical negligence are concerned. For more information visit the Forensic Science Service website at www.forensic.gov.uk.

FORENSIC SCIENTIST/ASSISTANT FORENSIC SCIENTIST/LABORATORY ATTENDANT

The forensic scientist is a more senior role than a scene of crime officer and is based in the laboratory. Candidates require detailed knowledge of biology, chemistry, drugs and toxicology, so if sciences are your thing, this could well be the career route for you. Much of the work will consist of analysing samples that have been taken at a crime scene – whether blood, hair, fabric or even paint or solvents – and intense attention to detail is needed because the forensic scientist is looking for the evidence to link a suspect with a crime. Forensic scientists are often called upon to report impartially about evidence in court. The assistant forensic scientist is obviously the next step down from this role, while laboratory attendants offer lab support.

FIRE INVESTIGATION OFFICER
You must first become a fully trained forensic scientist before you can receive further training to become a fire investigation officer. Fire investigation officers are brought in to ascertain whether a fire was lit deliberately, what was used to start it and where its point of origin was. Visit www.forensic.gov.uk for more information.

FIREARMS TECHNICAL OFFICERS/FIREARMS REPORTING OFFICERS
You find a spent bullet at the scene of a crime – how can you tell which gun it was fired from? That's where the firearms specialists come in. They collect, examine and classify weapons and ammunition. They attend the scenes of crimes where firearms have been used to deduce the trajectory of bullets (ie where they were fired from in relation to where they ended up) and can also calculate the velocity of bullets and how far they have travelled.

ELECTRONIC CASEWORKER
As technology gets ever more sophisticated, so too must the methods of examining that technology. CCTV footage, mobile phones and computers are now all fertile ground for the electronic caseworker, who looks for evidence to pinpoint a suspect to a certain place at a certain time or, in the case of computers, proves that they have downloaded certain items from the internet or committed fraud. This is painstaking, methodical work suited to those who like a desk-bound job, sitting in front of a computer screen.

SUPPORT STAFF

The police force could not function efficiently without its many support staff. These are the administrators and secretarial staff who make sure the whole operation works on a day-to-day basis. Apart from general clerical duties such as typing and filing, advanced IT skills are becoming an important part of the job.

SECRETARIAL STAFF

Jobs in this sector include **clerical assistant**, **personal assistant**, **personal secretary**, **librarian**, **legal typist** and **national deputy secretary**. For all these positions some form of secretarial experience will be needed before joining the force.

Other positions include **call handler** and **call controller**, both of whom will operate out of a call centre and be responsible for responding to calls received.

Finally, the **analyst** and **higher analyst** collate and analyse information as a support to the police. Most of these positions involve working from offices and stations and do not involve being out on the streets.

OTHER SUPPORT STAFF

One section of the police support staff will definitely be working outdoors. These are the **traffic wardens** and **vehicle removal officers** who enforce traffic regulations, making sure road conditions are safe for pedestrians, issuing parking tickets and ensuring that cars in breach of regulations are removed. Traffic wardens issue fixed penalty notices and help police by keeping a look-out for stolen vehicles. They are employed by local police forces and currently there are approximately 2500 traffic wardens throughout the UK. However, numbers are now decreasing as many police forces are handing over the responsibilities of traffic wardens to local authorities, which employ parking attendants who have a narrower job description. In the London boroughs the work has been contracted out to private companies and in other areas there are plans to merge the duties of attendants and wardens into a single, privately employed force. Traffic wardens do most of their training on the job, though in major cities there are training courses arranged at police training centres.

BRITISH TRANSPORT POLICE (BTP)
The transport police force was first formed in the 1830s when railways became a major form of public transport. Our modern British Transport Police force came into being in 1962 and is now responsible for keeping law and order not only on the rail network in England, Wales and Scotland but also on the London Underground, Docklands Light Railway and certain tram networks across the country. In the year 2003/04 the BTP dealt with over 83,000 crimes (including homicide, theft and sexual offences), handled public order issues (such as overseeing large crowds of football supporters travelling to away games) and even suicides.

There are 2280 BTP officers (including 304 CID) who have the same powers as constables in the regular police. They are recruited and trained in exactly the same way as ordinary police officers at training centres across England and at the Scottish Police College. However, they do receive specialist training in railway operations, safety and legislation. As well as its officers, the BTP also has 221 police specials and 704

civilian support staff. More information can be found at the
BTP website, www.btp.police.uk.

ROYAL MILITARY POLICE (RMP)

Royal Military Police are commonly known as Redcaps
because of their eye-catching headgear. They are
responsible for investigating, detecting and reporting crime in
the army and in a typical year deal with over 20,000
incidents. To be eligible you must undertake training to
become a soldier before going on to do specialist police
training. You have to be between $17^1/_2$ and 30 years old and
do your 'Phase 1' training at the Army Training Regiment
(ATR) at Winchester. This lasts between 14 and 22 weeks
and it is only after successfully completing this course that
you can go on to 'Phase 2', the 21-week military policing

There are also great opportunities for travel as
the RMP force is based all over the world.

course at the RMP's own training school at Chichester. On
completion of training you become a lance corporal and
from then on there are plenty of opportunities for promotion
(you can achieve the position of corporal within two years) or
for going into specialist areas such as Special Investigations
Branch (the army's equivalent of the CID) or becoming a dog
handler. There are also great opportunities for travel as the
RMP force is based all over the world. A normal tour of duty
is three years at any one location with the possibility of a six-
month operational tour. If the disciplined life of a soldier
appeals to you and you like an occupation with plenty of

physical activity (there are opportunities to learn to ski, sail, parachute and mountaineer within the RMP) then this could be the job for you. For more information see the Armed Forces websites at www.agccareers.com or www.armyspecialist.co.uk.

As you can see, a great variety of roles are available within the Police Force, so there's probably a niche somewhere for your own particular skills and abilities. Opposite is a chart of just what you can do and where you could find yourself working.

A great variety of roles are available within the Police Force, so there's probably a niche somewhere for your own particular skills and abilities.

The Police

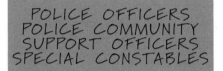

**POLICE OFFICERS
POLICE COMMUNITY
SUPPORT OFFICERS
SPECIAL CONSTABLES**

On the Beat
In the Fraud Squad
Dog Handlers
Traffic Police
Special Branch
Mounted Police

WORK

FORENSICS

Crime Scene Investigator
Forensic Scientist
Fire Investigation Officer
Firearms Technical Officer

WORK

On the streets, roads, football stadiums, city centres

At crime and accident scenes

In Forensic Laboratories

In cars, on motorbikes and on horseback

At Police Stations

In schools

SUPPORT STAFF

Secretarial staff (including Librarians, Telephonists, Crime Researchers)
Traffic Warden
Vehicle Removal Officer

WORK

On the streets

In call centres

In offices and Police Stations

7

BRIAN MCDONALD

Case study 3

POLICE CONSTABLE, ROAD POLICING DEPARTMENT, STRATHCLYDE POLICE

After studying for his O levels, Brian went on to college to do a two-year course in Building Technology, but he left when he realised he was not interested in pursuing it as a career. He had always had an interest in police work because of the varied nature of the job, so 17 years ago he joined the force. He started with the Metropolitan Police force in Peckham (south-east London) patrolling the streets as a uniformed constable. After nine years he moved to traffic patrol duties working out of Bow in London's East End. In 2001 he transferred to Strathclyde for family reasons and underwent retraining at the Scottish Police College at Tulliallan in Fife for three months. This was necessary because Scottish law is different from English law.

'I've always had a particular interest in traffic policing due to my liking for cars and motorbikes and all things mechanical. Once I was within the police service I knew this was the area of work I would like to

The most important qualities are honesty, trustworthine and reliabilit<

specialise in, so I directed my career towards achieving it. My current post requires me to undertake all the duties of any other constable but with special emphasis on the policing of roads. This involves such things as detecting road traffic offences such as speeding and drink driving, escorting wide or abnormal loads, reporting road traffic accidents and investigating fatal road traffic accidents.

'I enjoy the variety of work and situations I encounter on a daily basis because no two days or incidents are ever alike. There are always new situations to deal with and each will have a different solution. As my work requires me to patrol a large area and attend numerous incidents every day I am constantly working in different environments (be they urban or rural) and meeting many people from all walks of life. There's a great deal of satisfaction knowing that in some way you have helped other people who need your assistance. However, dealing with fatal road accidents and helping the families of the bereaved can be very traumatic and stressful. Also, shift work can have an adverse effect on your life especially if, like me, you have a family.

There's a great deal of satisfaction knowing that in some way you have helped other people who need your assistance.

'The most important qualities you must possess to make a career in the police a successful one are honesty, trustworthiness and reliability. On a more practical note a good degree of common sense will enable you to deal with most issues as you come across them. In the early years of your service you should gain as much knowledge as possible as this will provide you with a sound footing in basic policing skills. These will serve you well throughout your career. You should also gain a wide variety of experience in as many different aspects of policing as you can and then decide which area of policing you enjoy most - once you have identified this area, make it your goal to specialise in it.

DID YOU KNOW?

According to the British Crime Survey, the number of violent incidents has fallen by 36% since hitting a peak in 1995.

Source: BCS 2003–2004

'I chose Strathclyde to transfer to because it is by far the biggest force in Scotland, with around 7500 officers, and it therefore was in some ways comparable with the Metropolitan Police force in that it would offer me the best opportunities for developing my career. Having now been with Strathclyde Police for four years I think it has been a win/win situation as I have achieved the better lifestyle for my family and Strathclyde Police have got an officer with a lot of experience. At present I'm happy within my chosen field although I am now looking to further my career by gaining promotion. This will involve me undertaking a series of exams, followed by interviews and if I'm successful I would like to remain in traffic policing.'

8

Police: could you?

By now you should have a much better idea of what joining the police is all about and the wonderful opportunities it can offer. The detailed descriptions of the different positions within the police may help you to decide where you would eventually like to end up in the force, but what about the everyday conditions on the job? What will becoming a member of the police force mean to you financially and socially? Even more importantly, how will it affect your future career prospects? In this section we look at some of the most commonly asked questions about getting a job within the police and the benefits it can bring to you personally. This should help you to decide whether or not this is a career path you wish to follow.

WHAT COULD STOP ME BECOMING A POLICE OFFICER?

● Failing the application test for a start. When you apply you will be required to undertake the Police Initial Recruitment Test (the Scottish Police Standard Entrance Examination in Scotland), which includes an interview, a physical fitness test and literacy, numeracy and psychometric tests. If you fail this you will not be able to undertake the probationary training programme. There is a minimum wait of six months after failing the test before you can reapply to the police force.

- Although restrictions on foreign nationals from outside the Commonwealth joining the police force were loosened by the Home Secretary in 2003, in order to be an officer you must still be a British or Irish Republic subject, or a Commonwealth citizen not subject to work restrictions.
- You cannot become a police officer if you have a serious criminal conviction for something like GBH (grievous bodily harm) or a sexual offence.
- You cannot be an officer and play an active part in politics (for example by standing to be an MP) or have any affiliation with political groups that are known to hold extremist views: this is seen as a conflict of interests.
- The conflict of interest rule also applies if you, or your spouse or a relative living with you, has a business interest in the area of your force (say a shop, a gambling shop or a business licensed to sell liquor such as a pub or off-licence).
- If you have any visible tattoos that are viewed as inappropriate and could be offensive to sections of the public (eg a swastika) this could stop you from becoming a police officer.

ARE THERE GOOD OPPORTUNITIES FOR PROMOTION?

As we've already seen, that depends on what you want to do. Some officers enjoy frontline contact with the community and remain as constables for the whole of their police careers because they enjoy the variety of being on the beat, or because they want to move into another area (eg fraud squad/drugs squad) but still at the rank of constable. A constable's pay will rise incrementally each year (see 'How much can I expect to earn?' on page 58), so although they have not received promotion they are rewarded for their experience.

Because the higher ranks are filled from within the force itself there are always good opportunities for promotion. The next rank up from constable is sergeant and you must pass a qualifying examination to achieve this rank. Some constables decide to do this straight after their two-year probationary period, but most decide to get more experience on the beat before taking the exam (see Brian McDonald's Case Study in Chapter 7).

However, for those who are ambitious there is a High Potential Development Scheme (see Chapter 10, Training Day, for more details). If you have the right qualities and abilities this can help fast-track you on the promotion ladder. Some officers who join the police as graduates seek to take

Because the higher ranks are filled from within the force itself there are always good opportunities for promotion

advantage of this scheme because it is intensive and favours those with a strong educational background. The rank after sergeant is inspector and, once again, you must pass a qualifying examination to achieve this rank. Promotion to all ranks above inspector (chief inspector, superintendent, chief superintendent) is achieved through a selection process rather than by exam results.

WILL I WORK NINE TO FIVE?

As a police officer, most definitely not. The normal working week is 40 hours on a shift basis, although different forces around the country have different shift patterns. During the

CAREER OPPORTUNITIES

PASS POLICE INITIAL
RECRUITMENT TEST

TWO-YEAR PROBATIONARY PERIOD
AS CONSTABLE

EXPERIENCE ON JOB
AND MORE TRAINING

**TRAFFIC POLICE
FRAUD SQUAD
DRUGS SQUAD
SPECIAL BRANCH
CRIMINAL INVESTIGATION DEPT
DOG HANDLERS
MOUNTED POLICE**

GAIN MORE
EXPERIENCE

HIGH POTENTIAL
DEVELOPMENT
SCHEME

TAKE EXAM TO
BECOME SERGEANT

GAIN MORE EXPERIENCE
TAKE EXAM TO BECOME INSPECTOR

GAIN MORE EXPERIENCE. PASS SELECTION
PROCESS TO BECOME CHIEF INSPECTOR,
SUPERINTENDENT AND CHIEF SUPERINTENDENT

course of a week you should have two rest days and if you have to work these days you should receive compensation. Overtime is paid as follows:

- For casual overtime, worked at the end of a shift without notification, you get paid time plus a third (although the first thirty minutes is not factored in unless you work more than four such periods in a seven-day stint).
- If you are required to work overtime on a public holiday (such as over Christmas or New Year) you receive double time payments if you have been given eight days' notice. (If you would prefer, you can forgo the payment and take time off in lieu instead.)
- If less than eight days' notice has been given you get double pay and time off in lieu.

Inevitably, police officers do have to work unsociable hours because they deliver a 24-hour service, 7 days a week, 365 days of the year. Someone has to police the Glastonbury Festival, the Edinburgh Fringe Festival, football matches and large rallies, most of which take place at the weekend when members of the public are relaxing. Also, if there is a major break-in or disturbance at 3am the police must be available for call-out. If early mornings, late nights and working while your mates are out enjoying themselves is a big turn-off for you then policing is not going to be a good career choice.

WILL I GET TIME OFF FOR HOLIDAYS?
Of course you will, and that includes the initial two-year probationary period. Police officers receive 22 days leave per annum during the first five years of their service. After five years this rises incrementally depending on your length of service. Women officers are also entitled to maternity leave,

three months of which is paid leave. Also, once the probationary period is over, in some circumstances officers can take what is known as a 'career break' of up to five years. This is discretionary – it will depend on your police record and is a matter for your chief officer to decide.

HOW MUCH CAN I EXPECT TO EARN?

Policing is a serious job with many serious responsibilities and the pay structure reflects this. Police pay is reviewed each year so the figures below (correct at July 2005) should only be taken as a guideline. When you first undertake your **training** the salary is around £19,803, rising to £22,107 once this initial training period is over. Year on year your salary will rise to around £31,092 a year. This is also the initial salary for a **newly qualified sergeant**, whose pay can rise to £34,944 after four years.

Obviously, the higher the rank, the higher the pay: **inspectors** earn from £39,840 up to £43,212. If you are working in London then you may receive a London weighting – this is extra pay to offset the higher living costs in the capital. For example, in London, inspectors' pay starts at £41,586 and rises to £44,970. You can, of course, earn more by working overtime, but this will obviously depend on an individual's own circumstances.

Police community support officers (PCSOs) earn less than constables as they do not have the same level of responsibility, but they still earn a living. How much they earn will very much depend on exactly where they live in the country. For example, PCSOs in Cambridgeshire earn between £14,424 and £17,000 (plus bonuses) depending on their level of experience and length of service, while those in

Derbyshire earn between £16,443 and £19,887. Because of the extra London allowance, PCSOs in the Metropolitan Police force earn between £17,789 and £20,448.

Special constables are volunteers so they do not earn a salary, but they do receive travel and other expenses and their uniform is provided free. Some forces also provide local allowances: check with individual forces for details of these.

Crime scene investigators have a starting salary of £16,280, and this can rise to more than £35,000 for **senior crime scene examiners**.

As far as police support staff are concerned **traffic wardens** earn between £14,000 and £17,000, while a recent advertisement for **performance analysts** for the Metropolitan Police indicated starting salaries of £20,653 rising to £43,132, with an additional £2864 available for a **senior performance analyst** (source: the *Evening Standard* jobs supplement, 'esjobs').

WHAT ABOUT FUTURE FINANCIAL SECURITY?

There is a Police Pension Scheme you join automatically when you become an officer, although you can choose to make other arrangements. You can even transfer pension contributions you have made from previous employment into the police scheme. The contribution rate is quite high at 11% of pensionable pay and most officers are eligible to collect their pension when they reach 50 years of age and have 25 years of service under their belt. If you have served 30 years but are under 50 years old, you are also eligible to collect your pension.

WILL I BE ABLE TO USE MY SKILLS ABROAD?

Some police officers already are. If you read Chapter 1
(Metropolitan Police Commissioner Sir Ian Blair's success
story) you will have seen that there are Met officers working
on the ground in Iraq and in Afghanistan, helping to train the
new police forces in those countries. Other officers travel
overseas in connection with cases they are working on.
However, these are exceptions rather than the norm. A
better question to ask is 'Will I be able to move from force to
force in England and Scotland?' The answer is yes, in most
cases you will. Some officers may wish to move from a small
county force to a big metropolitan force in order to gain
more experience; others may wish to move from the city to a
more rural force when they start a family. A successful
transfer request will very much depend on whether the force
to which you wish to transfer actually has any vacancies,
whether you have the necessary experience to fill that
vacancy, and your length of service.

The situation is slightly different for Royal Military Police, who
are posted worldwide, so you could well find yourself
working abroad.

WILL I BE ABLE TO CHOOSE WHERE I WORK AND LIVE?

Where you work will depend on which force you choose to
join. Many probationers choose to join and train with forces
in the area they grew up in simply because they have family
and friends there and they know their way around. Once you
have joined a force you will be required to perform your
duties anywhere within the area that force operates, so you
could find yourself moving around within your specific
locality. This is something over which you will not necessarily

have control – for example, PC James Kew (Chapter 5) of the Metropolitan Police was 'compulsory tendered' (transferred) from Mitcham in the borough of Merton to Brixton in the borough of Lambeth when there was a shortage of officers there. This degree of flexibility is one of the things many police officers actually like about joining the force. As an officer you have to find your own accommodation and this must be approved by the chief officer of your force.

WHAT CAN I EXPECT TO GET OUT OF THE JOB PERSONALLY?

In short, some extremely professional training that will enable you to deal with all sorts of people and situations. This training will give you a sense of actually making a difference to the community you live in and the knowledge that ordinary people are reassured by your presence. From the little old lady who is anxious about going to the shops to the witness to a crime who needs your protection, the very fact that you are there in uniform and have sworn to preserve

The very fact that you are there in uniform and have sworn to preserve order and prevent crime is a major contribution to the sense of wellbeing in society as a whole.

order and prevent crime is a major contribution to the sense of wellbeing in society as a whole. This is especially important at a time when public order and its perceived breakdown is a political hot potato. Being the visible face of crime prevention makes you the link between the forces of law and ordinary citizens. At the end of the day you can feel satisfied that you are making a contribution to cutting crime and making our streets and roads a safer place to be.

Another added bonus is the camaraderie you experience with your fellow officers. Not only will you be spending a lot of time with them during working hours but they are also the men and women you rely on for your safety during difficult situations, and friendships forged within the force can last a lifetime. Many forces have their own sports and social clubs (such as football, rugby, running and tennis), so a social life in the police can be a rich and varied one.

HOW WILL THE WIDER PUBLIC VIEW ME?

There will always be a section of the public that does not like the police – however, this tends to be the section that frequently breaks the law! Doing this job you are never going to be the friend of the carjacker or persistent thief, but on the whole the public will see you as enormously valuable. Even today, police officers are seen as figures of authority, and when law and order breaks down, the public looks to them to restore the status quo. If your home is broken into, your car stolen or you are mugged for your mobile phone then the police are the first port of call. We look to them for reassurance, comfort and protection. The public perceives the police as its guard against lawlessness and this is not a responsibility to take lightly.

JONATHAN MORRISON

Case study 4

9

SAFER SCHOOLS OFFICER

Jonathan is black and, as a child, he never even thought about joining the police force because he considered it a racist organisation. However, one day while he was watching television, he saw a programme in which a black police officer was talking very honestly, on their level, to a group of young people, and he changed his mind. Although he had not done well at school (he was easily distracted and got into trouble for fighting), he applied to join the force and was successful. Jonathan, who is now 29, works as a Safer Schools Officer in Lewisham. He is also one of the police officers involved in presenting the TV programme *Crimewatch*.

'My role as a Safer Schools Officer involves speaking to young people between the ages of seven and eleven years old and diverting them from potential trouble. I give lessons on crime and the consequences of their actions, bridging the gap between them and the police and hopefully breaking down barriers. I like helping young people not to make the same mistakes I did and I try my best to keep them in education and

My best piece of advice for anyone wanting to join the police, regardless of race, is 'be yourself'!

away from crime. However, one of the downsides of what I do is when I can't help them. Also, my job is not seen as "important" by many other people in the service and I do find that disheartening.

'My best piece of advice for anyone wanting to join the police, regardless of race, is *"be yourself!"* Don't get

You have to be honest and have integrity and you need to actually care about people and want to help them.

assimilated into the organisation and lose your identity. You will be much more of an asset to the whole police organisation if you stay true to who you are. You have to be honest and have integrity and you need to actually care about people and want to help them. If you are serious about joining then see for yourself what it is like. Don't get second-hand information about the police. Make up your own mind. You'll soon realise that we are a great organisation and one that can only get better by having more black officers.

'I really like being a Safer Schools Officer, but I am ambitious and I want to get promoted so I will eventually have to leave this position. Ultimately, I would like to be the first black Commissioner of the Metropolitan Police force.'

Training day

10

So now you've really decided that joining the police force is what you want to do, what's the next step? Well, first you must check you are eligible. You must be over 18$^{1}/_{2}$ years old to join and you have to be a British, Irish or Commonwealth citizen in order to become an officer. You will also be asked about your own police record – if you have been convicted of a serious crime it is highly unlikely you will even be considered. The good news, however, is that there are no set academic standards for entry across the board into the service. You certainly don't have to be a graduate, although many people do join after taking a degree. Some forces will ask for specific grades at GCSE in some basic subjects (eg English/maths), but most are much more interested in the results of the Police Initial Recruitment educational, medical and fitness tests (or the Scottish Police Standard Entrance Examination in Scotland), which they set themselves and which every prospective candidate has to pass.

Some forces will ask for a full driving licence (or proof that you are learning to drive). Both the Greater Manchester Police and the West Midlands Police have developed Pre-recruitment Access courses running at local colleges to help would-be candidates, so check their websites for more details (see Chapter 13, Resources).

First you must decide which force around the country you want to join. Then write to it for an application form (see Resources for web addresses). You must complete and return the form, and if your application is successful you will be given a date to attend an assessment centre. It is here that you will undergo an interview, written tests in English and maths, role-play tests and medical and fitness tests. You will also be asked for references and you must pass a security check. Only when you have passed all of these will you be offered a place on the two-year Probationer Training Course (PTC). This initial training must be completed on a full-time basis and you will be paid from £19,803 on commencing your training to £22,107 on completion of the training period, and will be eligible for 22 days' annual leave per year of your training.

DID YOU KNOW?

In spring 2005, the Mayor of London's office revealed its budget for the coming year. It included provision for an extra 900 police officers for the capital.

Source: Mayor of London's Office

PROBATIONER TRAINING COURSE (PTC)

There may well be changes to the PTC in coming years. This is because a new programme of training known as the Initial Police Learning and Development Programme (IPLDP) is currently being piloted as part of the Government's modernisation programme for the police services throughout England and Wales. However, any restructuring of the PTC is not likely to be implemented straight away and at the time of going to press the following PTC was in place. Prospective recruits will need to contact their local force to find out what training programme they run. Please note that some forces (such as the Metropolitan Police) work to a slightly different timetable.

access to

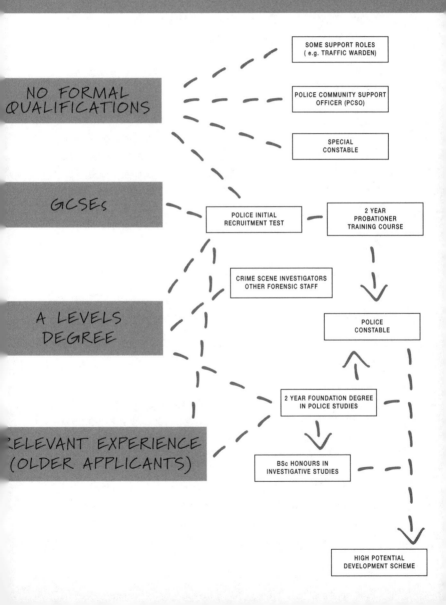

NO FORMAL
QUALIFICATIONS

SOME SUPPORT ROLES
(e.g. TRAFFIC WARDEN)

POLICE COMMUNITY SUPPORT
OFFICER (PCSO)

SPECIAL
CONSTABLE

GCSEs

POLICE INITIAL
RECRUITMENT TEST

2 YEAR
PROBATIONER
TRAINING COURSE

CRIME SCENE INVESTIGATORS
OTHER FORENSIC STAFF

A LEVELS
DEGREE

POLICE
CONSTABLE

2 YEAR FOUNDATION DEGREE
IN POLICE STUDIES

RELEVANT EXPERIENCE
(OLDER APPLICANTS)

BSc HONOURS IN
INVESTIGATIVE STUDIES

HIGH POTENTIAL
DEVELOPMENT SCHEME

STAGE ONE

This is known as the Introduction to Policing and usually takes place within your chosen police force rather than at a training centre. It is designed to give you a basic understanding of what being a police officer actually entails and how you can give the best service to the public. This stage lasts a minimum of two weeks but some forces extend it to include driving courses.

STAGE TWO

At this stage you will transfer to a specialist training centre, which is usually attended on a residential basis. Some forces may have non-residential places available but you need to check when you first apply. Stage Two lasts between twelve and fifteen weeks and is quite intensive. You will learn about the law and the core skills an officer needs to deal with a whole range of different police procedures.

There may now be some time off for annual leave.

The tutor constable is there to help and advise you with any queries or difficulties you may have.

STAGE THREE

Prior to going out on patrol you will go back to your own force to learn about procedures in your locality and you will also study your own community in greater detail. This usually lasts for two weeks.

STAGE FOUR

This is where you get your first opportunity to meet the public face-to-face. Working with a trained tutor constable you will be allowed out on patrol for ten weeks, putting what you have learned into practice. The tutor constable is there to help and advise you with any queries or difficulties you may have.

STAGE FIVE

You will learn about local policing for a further two weeks while your tutor constable will be consulted to see if they feel you are ready for independent patrol. If you are, well done! If not, you will receive further tutoring until you are deemed competent enough to patrol independently.

STAGE SIX

You should now be out on the streets, continuing to learn 'on the job'. However, you will still need to complete a further thirty days' training (minimum) and to be assessed in terms of your knowledge and your competence before you have successfully passed your two-year PTC, at which point you become a fully fledged police constable and your pay will rise accordingly (see Chapter 8).

FOUNDATION DEGREE IN POLICE STUDIES

If you are academically minded you can now take advantage of a new two-year Foundation degree in Police Studies, being piloted at five locations in England and Wales (including Teesside University, Canterbury Christ Church University College and the Metropolitan Police in London). Like other recruits, you will first have to pass the Police Initial Recruitment tests before becoming eligible to take the Foundation degree. Further academic entry requirements may apply (you will need either three A levels or a degree in another discipline), or alternatively your work experience may be taken into account if you are a more mature applicant.

The first year of the degree course takes place mainly in the classroom and includes civilian as well as police trainers. The second year sees students head onto the streets, (first on tutored patrols, then handling independent patrols) while also working on assignments and doing university exams. It is hoped that the more intensive work done in the university classroom rather than a police training centre will make for more fully rounded officers. After successful completion of this Foundation degree, graduates have the option of undertaking further part-time study and progressing to a BSc (Hons) degree in Investigative Studies.

HIGH POTENTIAL DEVELOPMENT SCHEME (HPD)

Whether you undertake the two-year Foundation degree or the two-year Probationer Training Course, there is the possibility of fast-tracking your career through the High Potential Development Scheme. This is designed for new trainees and newly trained constables who show they have real talent and ambition. There is a box on the initial police application form you need to tick if you think HPD could be for you. If your initial application is successful you will subsequently be sent an HPD application form and, once again, if successful you will then be fast-tracked. If you do exceptionally well during your initial assessment or during your probationer period but you didn't tick the HPD box when you made your application you will be sent a HPD form automatically. Although the HPD scheme is not specifically geared to graduates, it is very intensive and quite academic, so those with good educational grades tend to do well. Everyone who successfully gains access to the HPD scheme has automatic access to the HPD MSc in Policing and Leadership, and there are also other higher education opportunities. Sponsorship of up to £6000 is available to fund these courses.

Do bear in mind that higher-ranking officers are promoted from within the police service itself, so if you don't pursue the HPD scheme there will still be plenty of opportunities to move up the police career ladder by taking the necessary examinations. If that does not appeal, you can always move sideways by specialising in a specific branch of policing such as dog handling or the fraud squad.

As you can see, training to be a police constable is just as interesting, varied and challenging as actually being a constable. It's a mixture of both the academic and the practical and is designed to produce a modern police force that can face the challenges of twenty-first-century society head-on. In the next chapter you can read about how one trainer and one successful trainee feel about their roles within the police force.

11

LOUISE McCARON PC, RECRUIT TRAINER & KAREN KILLICK, PROBATIONER

Case studies 5 and 6

LOUISE MCCARRON, RECRUIT TRAINER

Louise was 23 when she left Ireland to join the Metropolitan Police. She has worked all over London since then: in West Hampstead and King's Cross she was attached to the Vice Unit. From there she went to Shoreditch and Hackney where she was specially trained to take statements from victims of rape and serious sexual assaults. Although she enjoyed what she did, after a while she felt she needed to change direction for her own welfare and development. Having assisted on some street duties courses she decided she would like to get into training, so four years ago, when she was 36, she undertook a two-week foundation training course. Since then she has been a Recruit Trainer at Hendon.

'Sometimes I see recruits who have harboured an ambition to be a police

Police officers are nurses, social workers, referees, athletes, teachers and advisers. It's not all about nicking people.

officer all their lives but they are never going to make it and that is very difficult because I don't want to completely squash their ambitions. Sometimes you have to tell them, either for their own sake or for the sake of the public, that they should think about doing something else. It's very rarely to do with their academic achievements but much more to do with their personality because they want the job for all the wrong reasons. Having said that, I love the fact that as a trainer you just never know what you are going to get. The syllabus is very similar every 18 weeks but the students never cease to amaze me: every now and then you get someone who is so exceptional they blow you away.

'In order to do this (policing) you should actually want to make a difference to society – I know it sounds very cheesy, but that's what it should be about. Ask yourself honestly how good you would be with a child or woman who had just been seriously assaulted, or if you had to tell a family about a sudden death?

'One piece of advice I'd give to all would-be recruits is you should always expect the unexpected. Police officers are a mix of so many different things – they are nurses, social workers, referees, athletes, teachers and advisers. It's certainly not all about nicking people. There are some officers (we call them 'thief takers') who have a gift for catching and convicting criminals, whereas I'd have to literally trip over a bank robber in order to nick him. That doesn't mean I'm not a good copper because what makes a good copper is a person with the ability to do everything. Someone has to do the mundane things like taking the dreary statements from the not-so-sexy jobs. Someone has to go into the house where a body has been lying for six months. It can't all be about rushing around in fast cars.

'If you are seriously thinking about doing this then you really need to explore exactly what it is all about and it's certainly not all about glamour or cuffing people or being involved in rucks. You need to know what will be expected of you and that you cannot go straight from training school to being a detective. You have to have that two-year probationary period, but once that is over the job really does open up for you. That's why working for the police is so good – because there is nothing you cannot do; you can do absolutely anything in this job.'

KAREN KILLICK, PROBATIONER

Although Karen's parents had both wanted to join the police they never actually did, and it is their daughter who has finally made it to become a police constable. She had always known it was something she might like to do when she grew up but as she was good at languages she worked in business travel when she left school. Three years ago, at the age of 23, she attended a Metropolitan Police open day and decided to apply to join. She was successful and started her 18-week induction course at Hendon Police Training Centre in January 2005. When interviewed for this book she was in her final week there, looking forward to her passing-out ceremony. She is now doing her two years' probation at Waltham Forest.

You can't come into this job with any preconceptions about people. You also need to be hard-working.

'It was the happiest day of my life when I knew I had been accepted to join the police. However, giving up my job was scary because I was quite secure there and was confident I knew what I was doing and that I had the ability to do it. I was moving from a safe nine-to-five job to a career where I had to learn different shift patterns and meet loads of new people in different scenarios; so that was quite frightening.

'Having said that, one of the things I like the most about being in the police is meeting different people from lots of different backgrounds. I also like putting the uniform on and going out and actually doing what I've always wanted to do – it's a really good feeling. The worst thing has been getting back into studying because at 26 I hadn't done it for such a long time and that has been the hardest thing about my training.

'The course is residential and while we've been here we've done loads of different things. There have been lots of role-plays where we've gone through different situations such as theft, domestic violence or road traffic accidents, and we've had loads of different presentations. We've also been to our Gravesend establishment where we did public order training in which we learned how to police a riot. We've also covered loads of different subjects including all aspects of the law.

'To be good at policing you need to be approachable so that people feel OK about coming up to you and you have to be open-minded as well. You can't come into this job with any preconceptions about people. You also need to be hard-working.

'My best piece of advice for anyone thinking about joining the police would be to go to an open day like I did and speak to people who are already doing the job – ask all the questions you can possibly think of. It was at the open day I attended that I suddenly realised just how varied police work could be.

'If you are serious about joining the police you really need to take into account that you will be working shifts while your friends work nine to five so you will be leading completely different lives. When I found out I had been accepted into training, lots of people said "you'll lose your friends; people will treat you differently" – but if they are really your friends they won't: they'll understand.'

12

The last word

If you've gone to the trouble of picking this book up in the first place then you must have some interest in finding out what being a member of Britain's police force actually entails. If what you have read has shattered any illusions you may have had about this being a glamorous and exciting career, that's probably a good thing: you'll now know that there is no place in today's police for people who want to speed about in fast cars, throwing suspects across their bonnets and shouting 'you're nicked!' in a mockney accent. Policing is a serious business and if you want to join the police you have to be serious about it. That said, it is a richly satisfying and rewarding career that can make you feel you have really made a difference to the community around you. Not many jobs give you the opportunity to meet such a broad cross-section of society in such a wide variety of situations and locations. There's also plenty of opportunity for advancement either through promotion or simply by moving sideways into a different division.

There is no place in today's police for people who want to speed about in fast cars, throwing suspects across their bonnets and shouting 'you're nicked!' in a mockney accent.

You'll already have read about the different positions within the force and about other jobs associated with policing if you decide the challenges of being a police constable are not for you. If you are still determined to join the police there are some practical things you can do while still at school, college or in your first job to increase your chances of being a successful candidate.

- Get some life experience. Do some voluntary work within your community, travel and meet lots of different people, join some social clubs – but whatever you do, get to meet people from lots of different sections of society. As a policeman you will be in contact with a huge variety of people from different backgrounds and with different religious and cultural beliefs so do yourself a favour by familiarising yourself with some of them now.
- Join the Police Cadets. You can join from the age of 16 to 18 and this will really give you an insight into what the police actually do. It will also give you the opportunity to talk to your instructors and other people who are already working in the police and who can give you first-hand information about what it is like.
- Attend a force open day. Many of the larger forces across the country have open days throughout the year where you can go and talk to officers face-to-face about what their jobs entail. Not only will this give you a better overview of the police, but might also help you to decide which part of the force you would eventually like to specialise in.
- Learn to drive. Already having a full driving licence when you apply to join can be a bonus, and driving is a good life skill to have anyway.

- Become a police community support officer (PCSO). Although you will not have all the powers a police constable does, you will still be able to help maintain law and order and assist in many ways. This is a great way to learn 'on the job' and see at first hand what the police really do (see Chapter 13, Resources).
- Become a special constable. If you are working in another job but can spare at least four hours a week to work on a voluntary basis then you could become a Special. Once again, this is a great way to learn 'on the job' (see Chapter 13, Resources).

Today's police force has come a long way from the days of Sir Robert Peel's bobbies, but his original ideal of men (and now equally women) committed to preventing crime and disorder while demonstrating absolute impartial service to the law still rings true. If you think you have the courage, commitment and ability to undertake that service, good for you. The peaceful and continued successful functioning of our society depends upon it!

If you still think you've got what it takes to make a success as a police officer then just read the list of statements below (part of the role profile for student officers set out by the Initial Police Learning and Development Programme (source: the Home Office)) and tick all those you feel you could actually fulfil.

THE LAST WORD

AS A POLICE OFFICER YOU:

ARE EXPECTED TO CONDUCT YOURSELF
PROFESSIONALLY AT ALL TIMES ☐

MUST ACT WITH INTEGRITY AND IMPARTIALITY ☐

MUST TAKE PRIDE IN YOUR WORK PRESENTING A
POSITIVE IMAGE OF THE FORCE ☐

MUST BE COMMITTED TO MEETING THE NEEDS
OF THE COMMUNITY ☐

MUST DEVELOP AND USE THE CORRECT SKILLS
WHILE DEALING WITH PEOPLE ☐

MUST DEVELOP AND USE THE CORRECT
BEHAVIOUR WHEN DEALING WITH THE VARIOUS
INCIDENTS YOU ATTEND ☐

If you ticked all the boxes, CONGRATULATIONS;
you may well have what it takes to become a member of the police. If you
failed to tick some of the boxes, don't worry; why not consider another role in
the police, such as a community support officer?

SIR ROBERT PEEL'S NINE PRINCIPLES OF POLICING

1 The basic mission for which the police exist is to prevent crime and disorder.
2 The ability of the police to perform their duties is dependent upon public approval of police actions.
3 Police must secure the willing co-operation of the public in voluntary observance of the law to be able to secure and maintain the respect of the public.
4 The degree of co-operation of the public that can be secured diminishes proportionately to the necessity of the use of physical force.
5 Police seek and preserve public favour not by catering to public opinion but by constantly demonstrating absolute impartial service to the law.
6 Police use physical force to the extent necessary to secure observance of the law or to restore order only when the exercise of persuasion, advice and warning is found to be insufficient.
7 Police, at all times, should maintain a relationship with the public that gives reality to the historic tradition that the police are the public and the public are the police; the police being only members of the public who are paid to give full-time attention to duties which are incumbent on every citizen in the interests of community welfare and existence.
8 Police should always direct their action strictly towards their functions and never appear to usurp the powers of the judiciary.
9 The test of police efficiency is the absence of crime and disorder, not the visible evidence of police action in dealing with it.

Source: www.nwpolice.org/peel.html

13

Resources

GOVERNMENT BODIES

Bluelinecareers
www.the-blue-line.co.uk

This is the police and criminal justice sector employment site and has comprehensive information on job specifications and job vacancies. You can find out what jobs in the police and related fields actually entail and you can also conduct a job search.

Connexions
www.connexions.gov.uk

Connexions is aimed at thirteen- to nineteen-year-olds and gives excellent information on jobs and careers. Click on the A–Z of Occupations and you will find job descriptions and specifications for the police and related fields.

Could You Police?
www.policecouldyou.co.uk

This comprehensive police service recruitment site tells you everything you need to know about joining the police. You will find information on how to apply, which forces are actually recruiting, what the responsibilities of police officers are and what to expect as far as pay and benefits are concerned. The site also gives the dates and locations of various police recruitment drives across the country. Click on 'News and events' on the homepage for a list of future recruitment fairs.

Learndirect

www.learndirect-advice.co.uk

This site has been set up for adult learners and it has an excellent job profile section where you can find detailed descriptions of hundreds of jobs. It also gives a realistic indication of what salary structure is like and links to other, related sites.

OTHER BODIES/ORGANISATIONS

Volunteering

www.yearofthevolunteer.org

If you would like more information about becoming a volunteer police officer then this website is for you. It explains what the duties are and the training structure.

Specials

www.specialconstables.gov.uk

This website covers the history of the Special Constabulary and gives more information on how to join along with policy and regulations.

Police Community Support Officers (PCSOs)

www.national-pcsos.co.uk

At this site you can really get a feel of what it is like to be a PCSO: it gives news, views and updates on policy and actual individual community support officers' experiences.

POLICE FORCE WEBSITES

Police Portal
www.police.uk or www.police-information.co.uk/policelinks

For links to all UK websites.

British Association for Women in Policing (BAWP)
www.bawp.org

Set up in 1987 the BAWP actively works to promote the role of women within the force.

British Transport Police (BTP)
www.btp.police.uk

This site gives information on the duties of the British Transport Police and also on recruitment.

National Black Police Association (NBPA)
www.nationalbpa.com

Set up in 1994 the NBPA actively works to promote the role of black and other racial minority groups within the force.

Police Cadet Schemes
If you are aged between 16 and 18, you could join the Police Cadets to get a taste of what policing is all about. The following forces have Police Cadet schemes:

www.bedfordshire.police.uk
www.derbyshire.police.uk

www.gmp.police.uk (Greater Manchester Police. The GMP has set up a pre-recruitment Access course for those wishing to join. Visit the website for more details.)
www.herts.police.uk
www.lincs.police.uk
www.met.police.uk
www.southyorks.police.uk
www.sussex.police.uk
www.westmercia.police.uk
www.west-midlands.police.uk (The West Midlands police has set up a pre-recruitment Access course for those wishing to join. Visit the website for more details.)

Royal Military Police (RMP)
www.agccareers.com
www.armyspecialist.co.uk

Properly known as the Adjutant General Corps Royal Military Police. To join, you must first train to be a soldier before going on to specialist police training. The army also has a recruitment line (08457 300111).

POLICE FEDERATION WEBSITES

The Police Federations are the representative bodies for all police officers up to and including the rank of chief inspector. The various Federation websites have information on issues that are important to their members, along with the latest media news and publications.

Police Federation of England and Wales
www.polfed.org

The federation represents over 136,000 officers. It is not a union but it is always consulted when decisions on training, promotion and all aspects of police welfare (wages, pensions) are being made.

Scottish Police Federation
www.spf.org.uk

British Transport Police Federation
www.btpolfed.org.uk

Metropolitan Police Federation's website
www.metfed.org.uk

FORENSIC SCIENCE SERVICE
www.forensic.gov.uk

This excellent site gives an introduction to the work of the Forensic Science Service, the market leader in the supply of forensic science services to the UK police. Click on the Careers section of the site for detailed information on qualifications, duties, ways to train and even work experience opportunities. In this section there is also a Vacancies site.

For more information about becoming a forensic scientist go to www.forensic-training.police.uk.